LADELL

REBIRTH
triumphant
Comeback II

ISEEBOOKZ PUBLISHING LLC
LAGRANGE GA

REBIRTH TRIUMPHANT COMEBACK II

Copyright © 2018 by LADELL All rights reserved.

Printed in the United States of America. No part of this publication may be used or reproduced, stored in a retrieval system, transmitted in any form or by any means-electronic, mechanical, photocopy, recording, or by any information storage and retrieval system, except for brief quotations in printed reviews, without the prior written permission of the publisher.

iSeebookz Publishing LLC
137B Commerce Ave Suite 300
LaGrange GA 30241

Book cover & Interior design: Priscilla Sodeke
Editor: Yolanda Rowland
ISBN: 978-0-9995869-4-5

Poetry/Personal Memoirs

All scriptures quotations are taken from the King James Version of the Bible

First Edition: 2018

10 9 8 7 6 5 4 3 2 1

Ladell

OTHER LADELL PUBLICATIONS

Temporary Breakdown but a Triumphant Comeback

Still Blessed

Still Have Faith After Losing it All

REBIRTH
triumphant
Comeback II

NOTE TO THE READER...

While doing research on a "poem," I came across several definitions of Rebirth. The definitions described me and inspired me to choose the title of this book.

Definition.net defines rebirth as "a spiritual enlightenment causing a person to lead a new life." As defined by the search engine Bing, "rebirth" means to flourish or increase after a decline.

All the spiritual enlightenment from these definitions stuck with me. It caused me to lead a new life; and the areas of my life that were in decline, started to flourish. Rebirth is the most important piece of work that I have ever written. It basically sums up the past 16 years of my life. It starts from the beginning and follows my journey into the present day. May God bless those who read this book....

> *God is in the midst of her; she shall not be moved:*
> *God shall help her, and that right early.*
>
> *Psalms 46:5 KJV*

Introduction

I am a 40-year-old woman, a single parent, a CNA (certified nurse assistant), a teacher, and a student. I am a daughter, a sister, a niece, and a friend. However, the best of all my titles; I AM A CHILD OF GOD.

I was twenty-seven years old when I wrote my first book, which tells the story about my past. But, I didn't start at the beginning... I want to give you insight, and take you further, by going deeper into my circumstances. I want to take you to the beginning of my story which encompasses my previous books that are no longer in publication.

I want you to know, sixteen years ago, I had a breakdown. I allowed Satan to whoop up on me and I didn't even fight back. I couldn't. He had me physically, mentally and emotionally. He had my mind, body, and soul. I was headed to hell with a one-way ticket; I was the pilot and the only passenger. I couldn't sleep due to having daymares and nightmares.

Ladell

I felt alone when others were around even in a room full of people. Satan was happy. He had me right where he wanted me. He wanted me to think I was alone and no one loved me. I couldn't see the forest through the trees. I had a young child, I was out of work, I had let go of God, and he had let go of me. Satan sifted me as wheat, and I was near death. I knew I couldn't die, but I wanted to. In my opinion, both now and then, suicide would have been a cowardly way of handling things. This is my story…

REBIRTH
TRIUMPHANT COMEBACK II

Chapter 1

I am a 27-year-old female who, in the words of my Godmother, "Almost Let Go". So, please don't think what I'm about to tell you affects a certain type of person, age, gender, or race; none of that matters. You may know someone or may have experienced it yourself at one point in time. If so, my advice is that you LEARN TO PRAY, stay close to the Lord, and remember Matt 16:23 which says, *Get thee behind me Satan thou art an offence unto me for thou savourest not the things that be of GOD but those that be of men.* I write this to tell you...don't you allow Satan to steal your joy.

A few years ago, I experienced something that I wouldn't wish on the least significant person in my life; I had a total meltdown. I was working at a manufacturing warehouse in West Point, GA. I wasn't getting enough rest, I was stressed out, not eating, worrying about everything but the right One. I was depressed, and I didn't know it until it was too late. For those who don't know about depression, it is an overall unhappy, low spirited, and sad mood. It may last two weeks or longer.

WebMD defines depression as "A clinical mood disorder associated with low mood or loss of interest in activities a person once enjoyed and other symptoms that prevent a person from leading a normal life".[1] It is a whole-body illness involving your thoughts and mood; it affects the way you feel about yourself.

In Job 30:16 the Bible says, And now my soul poured out upon me, the days of affliction have taken hold upon me. In Psalm 143:7 it says, *Hear me speedily Lord; my spirits failed; hide not thy face from me, lest I be like unto them that go down in the pit.* In other words, my heart is broken, and my depression deepens. Lord, come quickly and answer me. Don't turn away from me or I'll die.

The night before I ended up in the hospital, it was too late for me. I couldn't do my job. A lot of different thoughts went through my head. I was scared and didn't understand why. When I got off from work, I didn't want to go home because, when I did, I heard something or someone calling my name. I was scared to go to sleep. My depression became so bad that I was afraid to be alone in

---

1   www.webmd.com/depression/depression-glossary

the daytime. You would have thought I was going through withdrawals had you been a fly resting on the wall.

Before I ended up in the hospital, a lot of things happened. I lost my home and I had to move back into the projects; I lost two jobs consecutively and then my car. I was working every night and I still couldn't make ends meet. Then, I started having trouble with my health. I found out I had fibromyalgia. It is a widespread musculoskeletal fatigue disorder which causes pain, poor sleep, headaches, stiffness, and muscle ache. I felt as though I was losing a battle that had no end.

Anyway, that morning when I got off work I got into my car; as I traveled down the interstate, I remember crying all the way to my friend's house, a woman who is like a mom to me as well as her sister. When I arrived at her home, I dried my face and went in to visit my friend. I thought it was going to be a normal morning conversation; boy, was I ever wrong. I remember sitting at the table trying to eat breakfast and I was talking nonstop. You see, she suffers from her health like I do, so she understood. Plus, we talked about everything. I told her about my nights, I explained why I didn't want to go home alone and the voices I was hearing. I poured my heart out that morning. All I could do was cry. I cried for a long time, so long until I didn't know I was still crying. I blacked out somewhere along the way. Yet, I was still awake; at least, that is what they told me. I didn't, and I still don't remember anything that happened that day. All I remember is that I woke up the next morning in the hospital. How I got there, and who helped me to get there, I couldn't tell you. I was told that my friend called my dad, and he took me to the hospital in Opelika. He said I cried all the way. I didn't respond to much of anything at the time or so I was told. I am telling all of this to let you know that I lost a day. It is scary having to hear from other people about a day in your life that you can't remember.

I felt empty and alone in that hospital room. I felt as if I was at the bottom of a hole, without understanding. When I became aware of what happened to me; I was told that I had a nervous breakdown and was suffering from Bipolar 2 disorder. It is one or more depressive episodes along with at least one hypomanic mood. It is difficult to recognize and is caused primarily by abnormal brain functions. It is chronic, recurrent, and major depression describes it best. In other words, a person experiences higher highs and lower lows emotionally, thus having major mood swings.

I was hospitalized for a little over a week. When I came home, I started to see a therapist. You may ask, "does therapy help?" No, not really. I just pray about my depression and take one day at a time. It took falling 50 feet into a fox hole before I began to realize what was missing. I left God and got caught up in the world; so, God left me. He allowed me to realize my faults and sins.

I needed him. He was all I needed, but at the time I didn't know that. I tried to handle it all alone, and that was my mistake.

Years have passed, and I am still praying and crying about my breakdown. These days, people who know me don't know what happened. They see it from the outside, not knowing the intensity of it all. I hear people say, "Get over it, and put it behind you," however it isn't that easy. Believe me, I have tried, and to this day I have a problem with depression. There rarely is a day when I don't feel like I was robbed. I am constantly thinking about all that happened to me. I know it was my fault and no one else's. *Working this out is a day-to-day thing and, you know what, depression is awful all by itself.*

While in the hospital, I remember a nurse who asked me how long had I been feeling depressed. I asked her if it was possible to be depressed for 4 or 5 years, and she said "yes". I had dealt with a lot, but who doesn't from day to day? It is harder for some people to deal with depression than others. I thought I was strong, and I kept everything inside. I kept it all pushed down for so long until my cup ran over and I exploded. In general, all the mistakes I made and all the things in my past, including my childhood, got to me. I didn't have God in my life, so I was doomed from the beginning. I didn't understand it then, but when I look back I do. I am a better person and a better woman. Now, I wake up each morning thanking the Lord for what he has done for me. I know God has brought me through a lot, and I still have a long way to go. I pray every night thanking God for all he has done. I pray to Him so I can continue to live right, and one day I can be where He is...in his presence. Every minute, of every hour, of every day, is a struggle, and I am aware of my life and my surroundings.

Let us continue to be in prayer for each other as children of God. For, God knows what we need and how to bring us closer to him. Be mindful of life; dont let life keep you from knowing God, loving, believing, and serving Him. Let Him be your guide to handling all that you find hard in your life. He is able to do all things. The Lord will be there for you, even when man has put you down. This is my testimony; I hope my words will help you to understand; *you are not alone.* There are others, like myself, who may have had it worse, but they succeeded.

I wrote poetry back in 1996, when I felt lost and alone. It was the beginning of my unknown depression. This one is titled *No Vacancy…*

Rebirth Triumphant Comeback II

NO VACANCY

She feels she is all alone
She feels nothing is going right
Especially not tonight

So, she remembers she has one true friend
Who promises to stay there to the very end?

So, she picks up the phone to call
But no one answers—no one at all

She tries again, and there is no dial tone

She wants to learn
But no one wants to teach
She looks around
But there is no one to see

She screams
But doesn't hear an echo
She cries

But there is no one to wipe away her tears
She feels like there is no heaven

She says how could it be
If it was God would see
All that is happening to me

She tries to take it
But just don't make it

So, she kills herself
Thinking hell would help
But when she gets there
The sign outside says

No vacancy

So, what is a girl to do if she can't receive love from you-know-who?

Ladell

It's 2016 as I write this, and at thirty-nine, I still have my struggles with life as we sometimes do. This all happened in 2001, but now I have learned to trust God more. There are times that I cry, times I have been lonely, and times when I have been scared. However, there has never been a day that has come and gone, since my breakdown, that I haven't been thankful. Thankful, that I came back from the dark pit of hell I was in….

Chapter 2

What is different this time around, 15 years later? Well, a lot. I won't repeat it. None of it. As long as there is breath in me, I will give reverence to God and hold on. I may sin, yeah, we all do, but I will never turn my back on Him. I was once completely lost and, at 27, I started my healing process. It is one that I don't ever think will be complete, but as each day comes and goes I grow a little stronger. I found my way through the storm. I found my way... through the love I have for children.

In October 2006, I started to sub-teach. A teacher assistant job opened up and I took it. From the year 2006, until the year of 2015, that's what I did, from Troup County to Chambers County. I liked subbing because I was never in one place for long. I fell in love with working with children. I was growing stronger each day, or so I thought; but, in 2011, my health started to decline. I tried to fight back, but I was losing again. This time, food became my best friend. Satan knew I was stronger mentally, so he attacked my body. The new year of 2012 came, and I was eating more. I began to get depressed again. This is why I never say never. Food was my dope. It was how I coped with the fact that I could no longer work. I started to carry around food in a duffle bag everywhere I went. It was like cocaine. I had to have it. I needed it. Food was how I dealt with things. My weight increased to a whooping 400lbs. I was diagnosed with diabetes and, with the last little bit of energy I had, I applied to sub for Chambers County and was granted the right. It made me feel better. So, instead of me eating all day, it was only half a day. I found that my love for children was how I survived.

In December of 2013, I had gastric sleeve surgery to help with my weight loss. I lost 100 pounds. It was not easy then, and it is not easy now. But If it wasn't for the surgery, I would have died. My grandmom was there for me every step of the way until she got sick in August 2014. She had cancer. I didn't ask what kind. I just knew she would not live long. She passed away in May, on Mother's Day 2015 at age 90. She had lived her life, some may say, but as for me and my family, she could have lived to be 104 and we would still miss her just the same. I know I do, and I can only speak for myself, *I miss her dearly.*

Whether the news is good or bad, I find myself wanting to call her and tell her. I have learned that each day that comes and goes it gets a little bit better. For a long time,

I was angry with God. My grandmom, she asked God for 100 years, so I felt as though she had been shortened by ten. I had to pray and asked others to pray for me.

I was taking it hard. *How could he? How dare he?* This was how I felt, but who was I? Who am I to feel this way? God had been good to me. He didn't have to let me know her and have her in my life for 37 years, but he did. So, after I repented, I prayed constantly for forgiveness and to never love man more than God ever again. NO one should be put before Him, and I had to learn that the hard way. Yes, there were consequences for what I did. I say all this to say that being a Christian takes work. It is a daily challenge and we all have sinned. Whether in thought, word, or deed we are guilty. So, be thankful in all things, and know God will never put more on you than you can bear; he knows what is best. Each day, I am so thankful for life itself and for it being as good as it is because I have seen worse. I understand that you must take the bad with the good by placing one foot in front of the other and continuing on. The road wasn't promised to be an easy one, nor was the walk. But God did promise a reward at the end of the journey if we are faithful. So, when we fall we should repent and try not to do it again. See, my minister says that sometimes God allows us to go on detours before we reach our destination. For a long time, I was on a detour to hell and never to return. I couldn't blame anyone but myself because we can only play the hand we're dealt. We must make the best of it and try our hardest to strive each day for greatness, and to reach that city of gold in the sky. Remember, we all have to give an account of ourselves. Mommy and daddy cannot get us there, but our personal journey will.

Rebirth Triumphant Comeback II

AGAIN

Again
I try to regain all that has been lost
Again
I ponder over my life
and what a mess of it I have made
Again
I wonder will it be better this time around
Not knowing but believing,
Having faith
The faith that I once was lost
Again
I try to regain all the has been lost
Again
I try to go on and not worry
But sometimes I get in a hurry
and try to rush God
Again
I fell I hit rock bottom

Again the Lord is on time
Again the Lord is on time

Ladell

TOO GOOD

Too good
No good

To you
To me

How could you?
How could I
Continue to be

Too good
To a no good

Brother like you?

WHY LIE

To me
To her

About me
About her

When you know
She and I know

You are lying
Why lie

When you know
She loves you
When you know
I love you too

Why lie
My love
Or should I say
Her love
Or are you

Our love

Ladell

TRUE

TRUE
Getting attached to someone is like getting into trouble...easy to do
But letting go and saying goodbye is too like trouble...not so easy
To get out of and to do.

TRUE
When one is attached every time the wind blows
You smell him or her
When the telephone rang you rush to answer
Because just the sound of their voice makes you smile

TRUE
So to you...I ask why
Why does it have to hurt so much to say goodbye
When all you can remember is his or her soft kisses and tender touches
All of which you will be missing

TRUE
When you let go sometimes a dark cloud show
It is like a thunderstorm on a hot humid summer day...
A long time coming...
Much needed...

And make you sometimes wish it would just go on and be over...
Over like the pain in your heart
Because the two of you must part
Your higher power is screaming new start...new start...

TRUE
So, to you I ask why
Does it hurt so much to let go and say goodbye

TRUE

Rebirth Triumphant Comeback II

JUST BECAUSE

Just because the first time you told me you loved me
Was one of the happiest days I have ever had in my life
When you said it I felt it deep down in my heart
And every time I think of that day I get sick to my stomach
Because you lied

You really didn't love me
You loved my and my and when I
So just because you said you loved me
Don't mean I stop loving myself
So just because I care
Don't mean my heart you have to tear
Into a thousand little pieces;

Just because you said I love you
When I and I
And now that I
Think about it
It wasn't your words I felt
It was your and your and when you
So I guess that evens the score
I love you too, then

Ladell

ALMOST HOMELESS

Almost Homeless
One day on top of the world living for only today
Not worrying about tomorrow and its troubles
Not realizing I was almost homeless

The Lord sent clues my way but I ignored them all day after day
Not wanting to see what was in front of me
Bills piling up; behind on my truck and rent is due again
Not realizing I was almost homeless

The Lord stepped in one more time and tried to get me to see
What was in front of me?
I was losing the battle, I was losing the war
Almost homeless he screamed

Lord I ask what do you mean
Just then the phone rang
It was a bill collector saying
"I'm calling to see when you Will be able to pay me.
He said this is your final notice The next step is lights out

Oh God I screamed as I hung up the phone
What do I do
The Lord called out and said Don't worry I got you
Thank you Lord I said I should have listen to you
Yes, this is true, but you heard before it was too late

Now we can get this thing straight
I was almost homeless when GOD stepped in
So, this battle I could win
And all I could say was

Thank you Lord again
For stepping in
I was almost homeless
Almost homeless I was

THREE A.M.

3 a.m. and I am awake again I thought I heard someone crying
When I got up and looked around I didn't see anyone.
I thought maybe it was my daughter going bump in the night.
I was wrong cause I found myself standing in the living room all alone.
Well, I went back to bed and by the time I fell asleep I was awaken
Once more by this small weep.

When I looked up there was this old lady looking down at me.
Before I could speak she said, "Be not afraid my child
For I have come to comfort you."
Me I ask:
Why me?
When you are the one I hear cry
It is you that keep on waking me up, I said.

No, it couldn't be, I watch over you, not you over me.
And when you hurt, so do I and the same goes for when you cry
And when you talk I listen and tonight you were crying so I cried.
You see, what so ever happens to you, happens to me, she said.
When I asked why...she said, the answer is simple,
We are one of the same, you and I. I was sent to be your helper and guide,
That is why, when you cried I cried, even though you never knew it
I have always been there, it's like when you hurt I hurt

When you laugh I laugh.
Well tonight you were in distress and couldn't rest
I said, wait, why show me it all tonight?
Why am I able to see you and hear you? I asked.
You called out to me, you were crying in your sleep
And each time I came to comfort you

You woke up and the last time you saw me standing beside you.
You see, I feel what you feel, and when things get too hard for you to deal
That is when I will take up the slack and have your back.
Remember, my child, each day that comes and goes,
I watch out for you so, never worry.
I will be here when you need me in a hurry.
So, lie back down and rest and know
You are watched out for by one of God's best.

Ladell

TODAY ALMOST LET GO

Today I almost let go
I almost let go
He had me in his wing
He had me in his hand
And not realizing I almost let him in
He embraced me as one of his own
Trying to trick me into believing with him I was home
Today I almost let go
He had me tight enjoying me
Holding me with all his might
But just as I lost my grip
God stepped in and reminded me
He was not my friend
With him my life would only be brought to an end
He reminded me I had so much left to do
I couldn't give up
I couldn't let go
God told me to stay strong and keep holding on
He said I got this
Don't worry because now that he had stepped in
I was really home
I was really safe
I just had lost a little faith

Rebirth Triumphant Comeback II

TODAY

today I took your hand
tomorrow you may need mine
we share in a great love
one that was sent from above
so today I say thank you
because tomorrow may be too late
to let you know It's you I appreciate

today I took your hand
tomorrow you may need mine
we share in a great love
one that was sent from above
because only God knew
how important to me you would be
only he knew how much our friendship would grow
and with that said my friend

I pray

our friendship never comes to an end
and our love never goes astray

because today I needed you
and tomorrow you may need me
and I want to be the best friend
I can be just as you have been to me
thank you my cousin my friend
I will love you until God's end

Ladell

I AM WHO I AM

The me you see on the outside
May not be on the inside

I am who I am without one doubt
So get over who you want me to be
Neither because I am not nor will I ever be
I just plan on being the best me I can be

Accept that, believe that, receive that,

I am who I am and that is all I can be
You see there is a lot inside in which I have
Always felt the need to hide but not anymore
I have learned to be free because
I am who I am and that is all I can be.

The me you see on the outside
May not be on the inside

I am who I am without one doubt
So, get over who you want me to be
Neither because I am not nor will I ever be
I just plan on being the best me I can be

Accept that, believe that, receive that,

I am who I am and that is all I can be
You see there is a lot inside
in which I have always felt the need to hide

but not anymore

I have learned to be free because
I am who I am and that is all I can be.

Rebirth Triumphant Comeback II

INDEPENDENT OR JEALOUS

You say I am too independent
I wonder is it your excuse
So that you don't have to
Admit that you are one sided
With your love

Jealous
No
Mad as hell
Yes
Maybe even hurt
But jealous
Never

Too independent
I will buy that
Just don't insult me
In your one-sidedness
And in the process of it all

Ladell

WHO AM I

I wonder
Am I the girl I see in my dreams?
Am I the woman I see when I look into the mirror?
Am I the child who wants to hug her mother?
The one who wants to be close to her father

Who am I?

I wonder
I am the mother that tucks her child into bed at night
I am the sister that says I love you
I am the daughter who wants to know she is loved
The friend that is true until the very end

Who am I?

I wonder
I am the one that wondered
Who am I?

THE IMPORTANT QUESTION

They tell me life has its meaning
I say I can't tell

They tell me things happen for some particular reason
I say I can't tell

They tell me everyone has a purpose for being here
I say I can't tell

The most important thing they tell me is

God puts no more on you than he knows you can handle
I say I can't tell

But... Evidently he knows I'm one of the strong
Because he puts so much on me till I feel I can't hold on

I have so much on my shoulder till I can't stand
So I ask one important question to my favorite man

Lord give me the strength I need
Guide me be with me
And most important of all
Please hold my hand

Ladell

TICK TOCK

This morning time kept ticking

As I was thinking

I thought about yesterday

Worried about tomorrow

And wondered if there were some way

I could have a better future

As time kept ticking

I never enjoyed the present

And it slipped way

If only there were some way

I could get it back

I would hold it tight

And enjoy it with full delight

And ask God to handle

The things out of my sight

PERFECT

Now and then I wonder
What it would be like if life was perfect
Then again, I wonder what perfect means
Is it all smiles
Is it all good things

Is it no tears

No hurt

No pain

Just laughs

Just sunny days everyday
I just wonder now and then
Then again

I don't think I can do perfect
Perfect means no troubles

There will be neither mistakes nor lessons to be learned
I don't think I wanna be perfect
Or have a perfect life

Perfect means blind and I don't do blind
I love to see and I love to learn

Me and perfect
I don't think so
But I do wonder
Now and again

Ladell

AMEN

Can I get an amen the preacher asks?
And then you hear it from the first pew to the back door

Amen

Again they all say

The next Sunday morning and again at evening service
That is well and all but there is six more days to say amen
And study the Lord's words but instead we put down our
bibles and go party hopping all over town
Showing up on Sundays saying

Amen

Won't get you to heaven

We must live as God lives and believe in our hearts
He knows what is best for us
As well as our wants
So next Sunday when you are sitting in church
And the preacher hits a nerve and you say

Amen

Say it because you live it

Say it

Because you walks as he walks
Talks as he talks lives as he lives
Say it because it is who you are inside
And be proud you know how to let it show on the outside

Amen
Amen
Amen

TODAY'S SOCIETY

Brothers and sisters are fussing
Moms and dads are divorcing

In today's society

Little kids are picking up 38's and have
Put down the water guns, they even skip school trying to be cool

In today's society

Let us not leave out the little girls who meet the sweet little boys
And have cute little babies; teenagers are having intercourse
They say courting days are gone

In today's society

Black men are beating their wives
They even shoot and kill one another

In today's society

Others are standing on street corners slanging
Thinking they are good role models

In today's society

Little kids are looking up to their role models
Meanwhile gang banging
Let us not forget about the ten and twelve-year-old
Who is drug slanging
Trying to be like the big boys
That eventually end up in the big house

In today's society

Why don't we try and change them
And our world while we can?
Before no one goes to the good house up above
Black people what is going to be our biggest downfall?
And eventually kill us all? Yes, you're right

Today's society

Ladell

MIRROR MIRROR

As I sit and look in the mirror
who is this woman I see

Day after day and night after night
I look and see

Yet still no answer comes to the
She looks like someone I once knew

Her eyes seems do blue
It is like I can hear her cries
Could it be possible we have special ties

Who is she I wonder
Why can't I remember
Why is that such a hard task

Can you hear me
Can you see

Please

Why won't you answer me
Or could it be because you are thee
And I you

She looks familiar
Like someone I once knew
I look in her eyes
It is like they are saying their last goodbyes

Could it be me...
That I see could it be

FACES

Many faces I see
And they all looking back at me
One two three
Girl boy girl
All in his and her own little world
Boy girl boy
They think education is a toy
Though some take it serious
Others not so much
Free is how it is given
It's all about how you plan on living
Those who take it for granted
May not live the life like those who
Take it to heart
I was always told, if it is meant to be then it is up to me
Especially when it is free
Many faces I see
And they all looking back at me

Ladell

DON'T QUIT

I pray that God's will bless you in a special way.
Your warm hugs and handshakes makes our day.
For this our friends and teachers, we thank you.
I pray that God has his way in your life and that you both
Continuously decrease as he increases in you.

There are many obstacles in your way,
The devil tries to show out each day,
But I'm asking the Lord to give you both strength,
And the ability to tell him like Jesus did,
SATAN get behind me.

Sometimes things get difficult and hard I know they are
So I pray he shelters you with his loving arms,
And keeps you safe from all danger and harm.
I know there are times you may want to quit,
But God says my child stick around a bit.
You must endure though you are unsure.
We needed a minister and you were sent,
And as the days came and went you decided to stay around.

Through all the ups and downs,
We have shared years of wonderful memories here
And all of them we hold dear.
Your wisdom is so helpful, as on God you depend.
May he be with you all of your days
And continue to use you, as we all give Him praise.
We love you and appreciate you for all you have done
As we look back and wonder where has the years gone.

Rebirth Triumphant Comeback II

RESCUE ME

Anger
Rage
Being overwhelmed
Feeling boxed in
Can't Get Free
Can't breathe
Dear Lord
Rescue Me

Ladell

GROWN MAN

My future is mine. It is not determined
By my parents' past nor their hopes and dreams.
It is up to me if it is to be.

I will set my expectations high.
I will live life with enthusiasm and purpose.

I think back to when I was a child and how I spoke as a child.
I did childish things. Then I went through a change,
As I became a young man I set aside all childish things.
I became mature, not so easy to allure into things of a child.

Becoming a man was one of the hardest
transformations I have went through thus far in my life,
Not only did my voice change but my body changed
Then my entire life changed.
Things I once had no use for became important to me.
I felt as though I crossed over in the blink of an eye.

I now think about future things.
I think about the places I will go,
The people I will meet and the woman I will one day marry.
I think of how I will take care of mine.
I will be able to be dependent upon,
I will stand, and I will be an independent man.

A man of discipline.
One who cares, have joy and love.
I will not only love and care for me
But those with whom I come into contact with as well.

My life will not just be my own, But I will give it to the Lord.

I will live one moment at a time. My goals will be achieved one by one.
And this is my plan when I have become

A FULL-GROWN MAN…

Rebirth Triumphant Comeback II

HARLOT

A pretty brown brown
has been all over town…

Up and down the streets…
She has heard lots of boy's heart beats
Even given away her treats

She has been turned out
without one doubt
It doesn't matter who…
So, watch out
Her next victim could be you

You have been warned
Everything that shines
Ain't glitter and all glitter ain't gold

Now she old,

But still lurks around the old neighborhood
Looking waiting and watching
Every man that comes by
So, she can say HI

Damn

A pretty brown brown
That has been all over town

Ladell

FORGIVENESS

As I sit back and think about my life. I think about how I use to be a good student. I was a loving, kind, sweet, kind-hearted and generous person. As each year came and went I changed. I changed into a kind of woman I never met before. Through this course of years, I allowed life to beat up on me so bad until it forever changed me. It changed me in a bad way, and I wasn't ever the same. Some say a change can be great. It can be for the better, but have you ever changed backward or in reverse?

I learned life will treat you like you treat it. If you choose to live it freely and full of bad things, one after another, all the time and live it full of lies, lust, and thinking we're in love, then that is just what you will get back. Lies, lust, and a fake love affair. It will kick you up and down and over and over again. I do agree though you get what you give. If you give mess, you will get mess every time. When I say living life backward or reverse, I believed I accomplished more from age 15 to 18 than I have from 20 to 35. Do you think it is possible? If you don't… I do. Instead of growing and blossoming, I grew and stopped. I didn't blossom at all. I messed up. I admit it. I really did. I did it all. The more I think about it the more I am sure of it. If I had not blanked or blanked, then blank would not have happened. As I think back, yeah, I am sure I messed me up. The only good thing is, I have learned and been taught even at 35, God forgives.

Chapter 3

HEAVEN BOUND

On September 26, 2004, I had a dream, and it was unlike any dream I have ever had in my life. When I woke up, I called my grandmother and told her about it. She said, *baby, you need to put that on paper.* Now I am glad I did. You see, my grandmother died in May 2015. It was Mother's Day, and since then I have felt as though a part of me is gone also. I told her I would put this in one of my books. Even though she is not here to read it, I know she is proud. Anyway, here is my dream...

It was about "Amen," making it to heaven, and seeing GOD, and having faith enough to go on.

One minute I was in a car, and the next I was walking up these stairs as if I was in a gym on my way to the top. I passed my grandma on the way up. She was sitting beside this lady. They looked so content and at peace. I went a little farther, and I saw my aunt. She was sitting, and I went on to the top of the bleachers. We couldn't talk to one another. So, I watched people go through the line, and it kept on going nonstop. I watched someone come and get a person as if they had to pick out someone and take them with them. I watched my grandma get picked. She got in and was able to go pick someone, so she went to pick my aunt. My aunt wouldn't go. So, my grandma picked another person and went on her way. I saw my aunt get picked again. She went to the door, but again she returned. She was picked again and returned again. My grandma didn't. She went to the other side where the lady that picked her sat. Grandma sat beside her, and they were content. Their faces were so clear and smooth and pretty. They were wearing their white robes and seemed to be singing. I could see straight across to the other side where they all sat. I just couldn't get there from where I was. See, you had to go through the door to the other side, and not everyone did.

Finally, it was my turn. This lady picked me, and she said, "I have faith in you."

She got me by the hand and lead me to this door. I went through it and I had to stand in this long line. I didn't mind, I wanted to know what was going on, and I was willing to wait to see. Plus, I wanted to go where my grandma went. I wanted to go to the other side. When it was my turn next, I realized I was in heaven. I saw Jesus sitting on the right side, and there were about six or seven more steps to climb, only you had to be lead up to them by the hand. I remember seeing God sitting in the middle, and I remember Him saying *You did it and now you may go and pick a friend.* So, I returned to the outside and got in the line. The line was for the ones who had made it, and they got to pick a friend and bring them to the door. You couldn't tell what was behind the door, but it had to be their choice to go through it. So, when I went back out, I saw one of my aunts sitting out there, and I also saw a classmate. So I stopped, and she said "Go on I am already in."

I kept walking until I got to my aunt, and I went to take her by the hand, and she said, "No baby, I gotta call my daughter. I can't until I talk to her."

She was not willing to see what was behind the doors. That was why she had returned twice. She wanted to reach her child. I thought it was sad, but I had to keep on moving and go on. I couldn't tell her what was behind the doors. See, this is where the faith came in at. My aunt said, "Maybe someone will come and get me again."

I don't know if anyone did. All I knew was I didn't have anyone to pick. So, I asked if I could see the LORD again, and I did. I told Him that I didn't have anyone to pick to help get in. He told me it would be this girl, and I would have to help her as she wasn't in heaven yet. So, I returned and I watched over the others. I didn't go to the other side with my grandma just yet. I was in, but I had a job to do first. I had not realized that when you went in with GOD if you came out, you were wearing a white robe. I didn't realize it while I was sitting out there wondering what was going on. Some people didn't make it out with Him, but they were not in with Him either. I will let you figure out where they went. So, until that little girl came, I was an overseer of all the other ones who were waiting to be chosen. While waiting, we had a feast and ate from this buffet. I did get a chance to fellowship with my grandma and all those others who got into heaven. We all had a blast. It was amazing.

I believe my dreams have a meaning and a message. What I received from heaven bound is that I must keep my faith at all times, for without it you have nothing for real; I have a job to do, and I must be alert and ready at all times. The Lord is using me and I want to be used. It is not easy to get through each day alone and that was what I was trying to do.

I learned to put all my troubles in His hands, and let Him fight my battles for me. I need leave it all up to Him. I think this dream was just a way to let me know to keep on doing it, and he will work for me if I work for Him.

Fast forward to 2017… It has been 13 years. My grandmother has passed. I believe the dream was also a way of telling me that I wasn't trusting God enough. My trust was in my grandmother, and she didn't have a heaven or hell to put me in. By my trusting and having faith in the Lord, I have a better chance of going to heaven. I have to be obedient and truly believe in God. You see, I put all my trust in her. I made her my god. I know now that I loved her more than life, and I need to have that kind of trust and love for God. Man doesn't have a heaven or hell to put me in, and that goes for grandmama, mama, daddy, sister, and the rest of them. I know now, and I understand this through God's grace and mercy; he allowed me to see, before it was too late that I should always put my trust in HIM.

Ladell

A LESSON IN LIFE

The hardest thing to do in life is live. People experience different things in life; therefore, they learn different things. No matter what we learn, somehow or some way, you can find someone who can relate to you or you can relate to them. When you find that person or they find you, you should be willing and ready to share what you have learned with them. It should be easy to share your thoughts and to talk to them. You may have an overwhelming and strong feeling in your heart to share. If you are not sure you should share yourself with them, that is okay. Remember, God places us in people's lives and their lives in ours for a reason. The thing is, we don't get to pick and choose. Though, we may think we do… sorry friend, the choice is not yours or mine to make. It is all in the format of your life.

Some people get off their path and meet people that God did not place in their path. Those people can be helpful and they teach us, too. It may not be something we want to learn, so be careful! The confusion is, we push away people who are the main ones we need to share with. This person doesn't necessarily have to be a lover. They could be a friend or a brother; only you will know, and time will tell you what you need to know. So, be patient, stand still and listen to the quietness. Wait on the Lord to send your special message of what you should do next, now, and forever. You don't have to be religious or righteous to know there's a God in heaven, and He leads and guides us throughout life. Sometimes we get off the right path, and when this happens, He lets us linger just long enough for a lesson to be learned, or a person to be met.

So, remember, just as seasons change and they also come and go, so will the people in our lives. He or she might be the one you thought was special; or the one you thought you needed most, and then he or she suddenly disappeared. Just know this person was meant to come and go. They were seasonal and were in your life for their own special reason.

It is okay to go through things and go through them again before you learn your lesson. Each person is different and learns at their own pace. The thing to remember is to never give up, and to remember the old saying, if first you don't succeed then try...

Also, remember that many are called, but few are chosen...stay on path, and you just may be one of the chosen.

1. If you and I do our part, God's miracles will come in quieter settings and greater quantities than we could ever imagine.

2. What lies within us is greater than what lies before us. So, know even though you cannot reach the stars, doesn't mean you have to stop trying to.

Ladell

LESSONS IN LIFE PART TWO. A WOMAN'S WORTH

Learn to love yourself like crazy.

Know that you are better than that. It's time to walk into a new season of your life. So, stand up straight with your head held high and proceed.

A new year is beginning, and if you are 30 or older, a new you should begin also. Don't walk into a new year and season with the past hanging on to you. No matter what is going on, let it go before the next year comes in. Don't let it hold you back and weigh you down. It will not be healthy.

You may say it is easier said than done. As a woman, I know this and I know what we go through. I traveled the road less traveled and I have followed the crowd and took the most traveled road as well. Because of my experiences, I know that there are many choices in life, but it is up to you as to which ones you choose. The key is to be strong and virtuous at all times, and never get caught slipping. Stand your ground, and never settle for less than who you are. For you, my friend, are worthy to walk into your season free. Free from all that had you tied down and bound this year. Let the past be what it is: THE PAST. Enjoy your present, for each day is a gift from GOD, and don't worry about the future, because your present day just might become your last.

Learn to love yourself like crazy and know that you are better than that.

Shirley Murdock has a song that is titled, "I Love Me Better Than That." In it she says she wants her joy, peace, strength, mind, self-esteem, hope, dreams, and life back. How about you ladies? How many of these things have you lost, as a woman, for whatever reason? How long have they been gone?

Shouldn't you love *you* better and greater than the cause of your loss. Whether you were bound by a man, depression, fear, or worry... Love you better and greater than all of the things that have you bound.

I am a true believer in the Lord and in self. This is where everything should start: first, with the Lord, believe, trust, and have faith in HIM only, not in man. Man will let you down each time you put trust in him. Once you have placed all those things in the Lord, have that same belief, trust, and faith in yourself, so that you will be strong at all times. This way, you will be able to fight for yourself when needed. You must love yourself as God loves you, and never let the words or action of others allow you to lose yourself.

1. Learn to be alone. (Just you and Jesus)

2. Find yourself. (What makes you happy? Smile? What makes you...you?)

3. Give all things to the Lord. (Anything that is greater than you, (keep the first one or the strike out...keeping both is

redundant) and let it go). God knows what to do. He got you. Unlike man, God is always there.

4. Ask, seek, knock, and pray. (When you are unsure talk to the Lord. That is why He is there. We must seek him out, knock at his door, believe, trust and have faith enough to know that He hears all things, and will answer you, even if the answer is "no"! Be still and quiet, pray constantly, and know that he hears you)

5. Be patient. (Wait on the Lord in all that you do.)

6. Love God and yourself as God loves you, and love your neighbors also. Never leave yourself out. You have to love you. If you don't, how can you expect someone else to? Know you are worthy to be loved. Learn to love what you see when you look in the mirror. Love all of what you see: not just ears, hair, nose, or eyes; love it all. Love everything from your head to your toes. The Scripture says, in Proverbs 23:7 *"Whatsoever a man thinketh in his heart then so is he"*.... know you are just as beautiful on the outside as you are inside because you are worthy.

7. Be content... Learn to love and appreciate yourself for who you are and for what you have today, not for what you had yesterday. Don't dwell on yesterday; it is not healthy, nor should you worry about tomorrow.

8. Be constant… Don't change like the wind blows, stop trying to be who others want you to be. Do you and love doing it. At all times, be yourself around everybody, not one way with some people and another way with someone.

9. Stand firm, and stand your ground… Know what you want, what you will take, what you will not allow or put up with, when it comes to your kids, husband, friends, or family. Know who you are!

10. Know it is okay… From the things you have been through, to the things you are going through. Know it is okay. We have all had our moments, when we are going through things. Don't be ashamed. You are not alone, despite what others want you to believe. Know that it is okay letting go of people and things not healthy for you. Anything negative-let it go. Don't be brought down by things that are negative, and don't let people steal your joy! Remember, misery loves company. Know that it's okay to move on to positive people, places, and things. If people don't understand, then oh well! It is okay to let go and move on. Just know that going through things in life is natural. What is not natural is never bouncing back after you have gone through it all. Never be ashamed of what you have been through and where you are in life; because, nine times out of ten, you are not the only one and will not be the only one. So, do you, claim yours, be you, love you, and know it is okay no matter what others say.

Ladell

Do all these things, and you are bound to fall in love with you; know it is okay to do so. Plus, you will be happier emotionally, mentally healthier, and you will be able to say "Yes, I love me better than that, no matter what others have to say."

P.S. DON'T SETTLE! DON'T

Know what you want and don't want
will and won't….
give and receive…
so that you may be able to
have…
hold…
live…
and love.

I am a woman, so believe me, I know it is easier said than done, but just hold on. Believe, trust, pray, and have faith enough to know that God will work things out for you, and have faith enough in yourself to know you are able to do all things through Christ who strengthens you. You will get there. Remember, God didn't create the world in one day. It took Him six to do all He had to do. So, take your time to work on it, work on it, and work on it.

Everything takes time, so don't rush it. This too shall pass, but know if you don't try, you can't fail, and you won't know that you can do it.

Be strong, kind, wise, patient, and last but not least, be a VIRTUOUS WOMAN...

VIRTUOUS: Having moral integrity; having or showing virtue especially moral excellence, goodness and righteousness.

Ladell

MY CLOSETS CLEAN

it growed
it showed
now what do I do

                my secrets out
                      my closets clean

I got help
I am no longer mean

it growed
it showed

they didn't like it
but they have to deal with it

                the secrets out and
                      my closets clean

Rebirth Triumphant Comeback II

UGLY

To you

Not me

About you

Not me

When you look
What do you really see
Or can't you see

The me I am

And whether you like it or not

I am who I am
And I don't give a damn
If you think I am

UGLY

Ladell

IT'S OVER

Unchanging in nature
So consistent in the way you stroke
Sometimes when your eyes are closed I gag and choke

The way you love me in your eyes
You in mine I now truly despise
So if you're wise

You would catch on to my tone
Get up and take your black ass home

IT'S OVER

REALITY

Taking life for granted
While killing one another

Throwing away lives
While not understanding the reality of it all

Death…

Burial…

And No
Resurrection…

Ladell

A BLACK MAN

Out and about as she went round and round
All over town
A seed was planted onto lonely ground
But no nurturing ever took place
So the seed was left to chance

When the rain finally came
The seed started to dance
And grow at its own pace

Now he finally starts to sprout up and out
And he grew and grew and no one ever knew
The struggle and things he once had to endure
Now a young man and very mature

He is finally settled
Strong and on his own
Standing tall
Educated and all
A BLACK MAN

Rebirth Triumphant Comeback II

GOODBYE

I choose not to fight
Like a lion raging in the light
But I will go gently into the night
Quickly, quietly, I'll be out of sight
Out of sight
Out of mind
Crying over you for the last time

Ladell

WORDS

Can be deadly at times
Hurt worse than falling from twenty stories high
Can kill a spirit that is bound to hell
Can cut sharper than any two edged sword
Can't be taken back once have been unleashed
Can kill a self esteem
Ruin a reputation
Look before you leap
And always think before you speak

REMEMBERING LOVE

Remembering you
Remembering me
Remembering we
Remembering love
Remembering…
Long walks in the moonlight
Cuddling, holding, one another tight
Smiling while the mood is right
Loving one another with all our might
I am Remembering love…

AT 16

I…
I wonder…
I wonder just…
I wonder just how I used to act when I was 16
When I was 16…
I was fast to learn
Fast at catching onto the things
I read
I was smart at 16
At 16 I didn't think I knew it all
There were things
I wanted to learn
Because there were things
I wanted to know
I wanted to know things just because
Just because I wanted to know things
I…
I read…I wrote… and I remembered all
I remembered all just because
I never wanted to forget…

Rebirth Triumphant Comeback II

LOVE

The simple things you do says a lot about you
When you send me flowers, or we talk on the phone for hours
Or when you open my car door or say I love you more
Oh, how special you are my little dove
You are my gift from the Lord above
Oh, how I thank him each day he sent you my way
Each time I see you my heart smiles..
then the beat stops
then starts again
Only this time the beats stronger and faster and faster
until it slows down again to almost nothing and just when
it gets ready to stop for the last time
You kiss me and it starts up and beats all over again
So, you see you can never leave me ever
For I am one with thee
And you are one with me

Ladell

THINK

what if we were best friends
always from the beginning of time
then one day we were riding down the highway

had a wreck

and we both died in the crash
then the next day you came back as I and I as you
could you be able to predict what would happen to me
and could I be able to predict what would happen to you

or

would we switch lives
or would we start over as perfect strangers
think

THE LAST TIME

After The first time it happened I
told myself it'll never happened again
I was wrong
it did
after the second time it happened
I told myself it'll never happen
again I was wrong
it did
and when it happened the third time
I didn't say nothing
I got tired of lying to myself
I told myself it can never happen again
or I will just die
but it did
GOODBYE!!!

Ladell

A SPECIAL TASK

As she lay there in her bed with all
Sorts of thoughts in her head
She wonders if things will
Get better

She wonders when the pain will go away
In the meantime she must pray
And ask God to make a way
So that her family may be able to ride

And stay side by side
So when they arrive at their destination
It won't be any hesitation
They will have come to do the task
That their mother had asked

Which is watch over her in her
Time of need
Then God will see they are capable of doing a good deed
They know her condition and just keep on wishing
She would get better and it only took an instance
To figure out her task that she had asked

They realized it was time to pray and ask God to send an
Extra hand her way
As I stood there listening to them pray
All I could hear was them say…

She's trembling…having chills
God knows she's very ill
We try to watch her as she lay there sick
But for some reason we just can't look

Mama we wish there was something we could do
To take the pain off of you
We wish we could make the pain go away but
In the meantime we will pray and ask our Lord
To watch over you
Day after day

MY SISTER MY FRIEND

My sister my friend
So long it has been
Since I've said I Love You
Since I've spent quality time
Since I've given you a hug or
Just told you how proud of you I am

Over the years we've gotten older
And I've watched you grow
Never did I imagine I would Love you so
My sister my friend
I will love you until God's very end

You are very special and very unique
And only God will know how proud I am
To have someone like you in my life
Only he can put it into words

Time after time I've tried
And fell so I will just say Thanks
For all of the joy you have brought to me
For all the love you've shown me
For every hug
For every kiss
For every laugh and tear

For all the memories that I will hold dear
My sister my friend

So to the both of you I will say
May you always walk in sunshine with blue skies every day
May your journey be a safe God-given one
And your love never go astray

Ladell

OUT OF SIGHT

I am sad
Sad I am
Yesterday I wanted to die
Tomorrow I may wonder why
Today I just cry

I thought I would be fine
I was so sure
Now I am not
There is so much
I have to endure

I have nothing to say
No thought comes to my mind
With a reason why I feel this way
Day after day
Night after night

I try to think
With all my might
But the answer is still
Out of sight

Rebirth Triumphant Comeback II

RESTLESS

Tomorrow brings a brighter day
At least that's what the old folks say

It is 2am and I'm not asleep for all
I can do is lie here and weep

Hundreds of thought runs through my head
As I lie here in bed

It is hard to rest
For Lord I have so much upon my chest

At times it is hard to tell what is right
I look up and ask
Will I sleep tonight??

For it is five and I still don't sleep
For all I can do is continue to weep
Is this how it is meant to be
Is this all that is left for me

Have I lived my life in such vain
All I will only receive is
Heartache and pain

Ladell

SAFE IN GRANDMA'S LAP

Count the sheep they say
Yet still no sleep today
I wish my mind was right
Oh, what I'd do for a peaceful night

For I am very scared all sorts of thoughts

Run through my head
At times, wish I was dead
I wouldn't have to deal with the pain that I feel
I wish I could clap and be sitting in my grandma's lap

Rebirth Triumphant Comeback II

SLEEPLESS

Last night I could not sleep
For all I could do is weep
Tonight things are the same
For that is such a shame

To lie here and wonder why
To lie here and cry

Asking is this meant to be
Is this all that is left for me
Has my life been in such vain
All you see for me is pain

Lord I'm all alone

All my solutions and hopes are gone
Though I'm trying to be strong
It is hard out here on my own
I cried out and asked for help
No one heard my cry they just slept

So I decided to look deep in my heart
And try to get a new start

TIME

Did I hear you say
Time brings change
In due time my friend…In due time
Time is change
Change comes with time
You don't get one without the other
They are hand in hand
Hand in hand they are
Time changes things
And things changes in time
At least that is what I heard

It's just that, right now
My mind is blank
And it is hard for me to think
But in time my friend in due time
Things will come into view

I Promise You!!!
My Friend
In Due Time!!!

UNTIL WE MEET AGAIN

I just can't understand why she had to die
She started out just my mother
We ended up as friends

She held my heart in her hand
As I held hers in mine
Over the years
We shared laughs
We shared tears
She was not just my mother
But my very best friend

It took us time to become close at heart
And only one moment to be ripped apart
I thought we would be forever
It only lasted a short while

Then God had to call my mother
My friend
I knew it would be no other
She was the best mother
My best friend
Until the end

I don't understand
Though I've really tried
I need her now more than ever and
Just a hug and a kiss
She can't help me now

So I will say farewell
My sweet mother
My sweet friend
Until we meet again

Chapter 4

PRELUDE TO NEEDY…

You know, society has placed a label, I will say, on *father*. They are taken lightly when it comes to their children. A mom has the most responsibilities, well, most of them anyway, and as long as the father pays or spends a little time, things are ok. But, you see, I feel parents should be careful when raising a child. Whether it's time, money, laughter, or love, it all should be shown. Because, when that love is lacking, the children turn to the street for what they are missing, and in my case, it was a bad thing. Now, I'm a single parent struggling, trying to instill in my child what both a mom and a dad should be doing. I lacked the Lord when I was growing up, and I pray each day I will be the parent the Lord would have me to be, so that the cycle is broken. All in all, my father did what he did, and now he is a better man for it. Like everyone, we have our moments when things are rocky, but I wouldn't have it any other way. Through it all, I still respect him and love him, for he is Daddy, how can I not?

…To my daddy, I don't know where to start. You have always been in my heart. It was always easy to love you, but at times, you were hard to get along with. When I was smaller, I watched you and my mom argue, and my love for you didn't change. I loved you even when you argued with mom. Even when you would hit her, Daddy. I never understood my love for you. It has always been a continual love. One that grew as I grew. There were times we fought, and I cried, but that never stopped me from loving you. I even tried to, but the Lord wouldn't let me. Even when you gambled your money away and couldn't give me a dollar a day for snack each morning before school, I still loved you. I know now, daddy it was all God. He knew me even when I didn't know Him. He placed that love in my heart for a reason. For me to share it with those who are important to me, and to those around me who don't know love. I thank God, daddy, for you, and I know through it all you loved me too.

We have a bond that my child can't share with her own father, but I thank the Lord, you stepped in and picked up the slack. Thank you, Daddy, thank you. My heart bleeds for my daughter. Substitutes are okay, but nothing is like the real genuine thing. I wrote a poem about how I would feel if it were me. I know she is content and happy, but again, one day Daddy she and I will have to face that subject head on. When that day comes, I pray I will be able to fulfill each question she asks with answers.

Rebirth Triumphant Comeback II

NEEDY

where are you
where could you be
do you not wanna know me?

I have searched for you for years
I have searched day and night
Yet still you are nowhere to be found
If you are alive you are not in my town

Who are you
I wonder
Can I know you
Will you show you

I want to meet you
Where could you be

Why don't you want to know me
Like I want to know you

"Daddy"

Cause I love you

your child,
Needy

Ladell

STAND UP

Today is the day that you will start your next journey in life. You have been working toward this for quite some time now. Now it is here for you to live. This day will never come again, so be careful, and live it to the fullest. Dream dreams, set goals, and do your best to accomplish them.

Today may seem like just another day for some of you, yet it is so much more than that for others. Today is the first day of the rest of your life. There is so very much life has taught you. Now it is time to make good and valuable use of these lessons. Life has taught you well and so have your parents, guardians, educators, and even your peers. Sometimes you will be frightened or uncomfortable applying those lessons, but still, you must proceed.

Of all the days you have ever lived and all of the days to come, this is the one you have in your possession right now. So, live it like no other. Make positive decisions, because your choices today will help guide your tomorrow. All the things you have done and experienced up to now, have given you great and meaningful wisdom, or a lifetime of regrets. The choice is yours, so choose wisely. Choose this day to be the first of many days to come that you will prosper and be blessed. So, live today with all you have, and know that the choice is yours to make. Have courage and faith to step forward and live life the way you have been taught. So today, STAND UP AND PROCEED.

DIFFERENT OR THE SAME

Two different worlds
Two different loves
Two different stories
Two different books
Two different people

One you
And
Yes, one me

So why don't you see
All I want you to do is love me

Yes
one you
And
one me

Same state
Same city
Same life
Same story
Same book
Same page

Yes
one you
And
one me
One love you and me
Together forever

Yes, one you
Yes, one me

Ladell

I RISE

They beat me; they rape me then put me into their fields
I worked and worked until my feet ached
with blisters that were hard to heal

Yet still I rise

They didn't want to educate me
You thought I would be a slave
until I was bound to the grave

Yet still I rise

They pushed and pushed
until I had fallen completely down

Yet still I rise

They didn't want me to vote…said it wouldn't count….
said I did not have a voice and never would be able to be heard
or make a difference

Yet still I rise

I rise…much to their surprise…I rise
They couldn't keep this good woman down
I became educated…turned around
And taught their children
I rise

Now when I speak…
I am heard in every nation
Because I was blessed not only with an education
but with knowledge, wisdom, faith, love, and hope….yes I rise

I rise to all occasions…
Now I tell of my fall…but I speak more of
how I rise

They know they couldn't keep this good woman down
no matter what they did
No matter what they said I got three steps ahead

Yes, I rise
Much to their surprise

I rise
I rise
I rise

BE GONE

You fooled me into thinking
You were my friend
So I let you in

And I embraced you with all my tender love and care
Only to realize you were just like the wind
Here one moment and gone again

You left me without a say
Only heartache and regrets
Of the day you came my way
Now I beg you to leave and stay away

But you just don't wanna go
When you say yes I say no
Just please go
I don't want your friendship anymore

I regret the day
I allowed you to come into my life
And move into my heart
Now I'm smarter
And I know we need to part

So depression
Be gone
Find a new home

Ladell

BROKEN HEARTED

God created you
I know you have a heart
I knew it right from the start

You opened up and let me in
As if I were your only friend

But in the end you let me down
You kicked my heart all over town

I don't know what I did to deserve this
what I do know is you didn't have to use your fist

I feel it is now time for me to say goodbye
it is hard, but I must try

I feel it is the right thing to do
or someone here will surely die
so, let us try

because the right thing to do is say goodbye

DEATH COMES TO HER

death comes to her

why you may ask
she seems to have some kinda gift
or a very special task

when he comes to town some how
she always seems to know

he may not tell her who
but when and where she seems to know

he lets her in on when he will show
and the direction he will go

never does he let her know who
because they may be someone
she know

death comes to her

death will soon become her
he showed her the direction
and when he would show
never in a million years

would she have thought
it would be her though

death became her that night and
she didn't even know

Ladell

A BLACK WOMAN

Beautiful, Brave, and all different shades
a black woman

light brown,

medium brown,

dark brown

skin

a black woman
once quiet without a voice
unaware of but hopeful
uneducated but inspired about life

a black woman
became strong and
courageous able to withstand the abuse of
being pushed down and ran over

a black woman
now educated
made aware of
inspired about life
with ideas for improvement
now creative and powerful beyond measure

we became
nurses, doctors,
lawyers, writers,
and congresswomen
never to be uneducated again

a black woman

LOST TOUCH

Why does it have to hurt so much
Whatever happened to Mom's lost touch

How can I learn to love
If she didn't realize I'm a dove
A Miracle sent from above

I want to be loved
I want to be touched
If only she knew just how much

No one knows the half of it
Everyone takes it the same
I feel that is such a shame

Why can't things go back to the way they use to be
You know when it was just Mom, Dad, Saquanna, and Me

Why did things have to change so much
All I want is Mom's lost touch.

Ladell

I MUST

He says he loves me
He says he cares
He says I'm the only one
I say I can't tell

One day he is here

The next he is gone

And when he does I feel alone

How can I believe?
How can I trust?
I really don't know
But my heart says
"I must"

LOSE MYSELF

Do I have to lose myself for you?
Do I have to lose myself for me to be the woman that you want in your
Life
Would it be ok if I let go of me for you?
Would it be ok if I let my guard down and submit myself to you?
Should I?
Are you worth it?
Are you really worth me letting go of me?
I don't think I can do that
If I lose me then I would not be able to give anything
Do you understand that?
Do you understand why I can't let go and let you?
If I let go of me then I will not have anything to give and I may not want you then

Ladell

LOVE

Describe it

Tell me

the meaning of it

Tell me

what does it mean to you

Tell me
do you know it
Have you ever shown it?
Would you like to experience it?
Have you heard rumors about it?
Just go ahead and

Tell me

What do you know about?

LOVE!!!!!

WHOLE AGAIN

The love we once had is now gone
you left me here all alone
I have had to pick up the pieces
of what's supposed to be my life and move on

but I just have one question how do I
supposed to do that when you
took half of me with you

how do I get me back
how do I go on
when you have made me
feel as if I am mold on a rock

when you left me
a special part of me left too
and it was the best part of me
and the strangest thing is
I don't want it back

because if I get it back
you may come with it
and I don't want you anymore

i'm glad you shut that door
i'm glad you left me
I just hate you took
any of me with you

but then again I am glad
because it is going to be the thing that haunts
each day everywhere you go
everything you do you will hear me and my voice
telling you how much you hurt me

how you made me feel
the good part about it is
I believe I have already healed.

I have already moved on
the Lord has made me whole again

Ladell

WON'T BE COMING BACK

So many years
So many tears

Yet still so much love
Inside that I can no longer hide

And, perfect we may not be
You know you and me

But the love and the pain is real
Maybe one day my heart will heal
And I will be able to deal

With the fact you are gone and
Won't be coming back

Rebirth Triumphant Comeback II

I LOVE YOU SO

your beauty is like a rose
so, refreshing

your smile is like the sun
it lights up my world

your laugh is like music loud
but soothing to the soul

I just thought you needed to know
you are my world and I love you so

Ladell

LETTING GO

if letting go of it is easy and getting it back harder

where do I start
where do I go
who do I ask

about getting my life back

loving you is not easy
loving you is not easy
but I try
God knows I do
but sometimes you make it hard for me to love you

you make it hard for me to deal
with all the things you bring my way
you make it seems as if
I must do as you say

don't get me wrong

I know you are the man
but know I am your equal
I was taken from your side
and not from behind you
and I will not stand there
I will be treated with respect

and you will listen to me
whether it is now or you are going over it
in your head when I'm gone
you will hear me and what
I am trying to say

I want to love you

Rebirth Triumphant Comeback II

I want my husband back
because you and I have almost gone astray
the one I fell in love with and
the one I married

please hear me now because
I will not repeat myself again
listen to me take heed to the things I say
because you and I have almost gone astray

love you so

I love you more today
than when we first began
I know sometimes I make it hard for you to love me
but know I will never stop loving you

know that it hard being a wife
a mother
a daughter
and friend
I am being pulled in so many directions
until sometimes I feel it all has no end
just know I love you so
and I promise I will do my best

to be the best wife I can be
because, my love, you mean so much to me
my husband my friend

so—long has it been since I said I love you
since I have held you tight
since I have created you in the night
just know I do love you so

Ladell

WE WILL MEET AGAIN

He wants to love me now
but when I was in love
he didn't know love

and now because somewhere down the road

he met love

he wants to introduce me to it
what he doesn't know is me and love
we go a long way back

hello, hi friend

I see your back

but this time

I have to follow my first mine

and step back

don't be sad I'm still your friend
and believe me when the right man come along
we will meet again

Rebirth Triumphant Comeback II

Ladell's Thoughts

You have read my story, so there is no need to retell it. You have also seen my rise and fall, and by God's grace and mercy, I am here and in my right mind. I have a renewed mindset. The things that I used to tear me into pieces no longer break me down. It is a struggle, and I constantly have to remind myself daily whose I am. I am no longer of the world. God has called me out of the world and has blessed me with a talent for writing. I pray that through my writing, I will help someone else on their journey. Please stay prayed up and be blessed.

LADELL

ABOUT THE AUTHOR

Shamika Marshall "Ladell" is a native of Alabama. She attends Park Avenue Church of Christ. She is a certified Nurse Aide with studies in Early Childhood Education. Ladell is an avid reader who loves to write inspiring and motivational poetry, short stories and novels. Rebirth Triumphant Comeback II is Ladell's fourth book.

www.ingramcontent.com/pod-product-compliance
Lightning Source LLC
Chambersburg PA
CBHW030454010526
44118CB00011B/926